DEAR YOUNG MONSTER

CREATED BY PETE MACHALE

Dear Young Monster was first performed at Bristol Old Vic
on 22 February 2024. It was revived at Soho Theatre, London,
on 5 August 2025.

DEAR YOUNG MONSTER

Playwright & Performer	**Pete MacHale (he/him)**
Director & Dramaturg	**Sammy J Glover (they/them)**
Producer	**Jess Donn (he/they)**
Designer	**Cara Evans (they/she)**
Lighting Designer	**Hugo Dodsworth (he/him)**
Composer/Sound Designer	**Roly Botha (they/them)**
Video Designer	**Dee Dixon (she/her)**
Associate Lighting Designer [for Soho Theatre 2025]	**Conor Divers (he/him)**
Associate Designer [for Bristol Old Vic 2024]	**Katy Hoste (she/her)**
Movement Director	**Loe D'Arcy (they/them)**
Dramaturg [for Bristol Old Vic 2024]	**mandla (no pronouns)**
Marketing/PR Lead	**Pansy Studios**
Technical Stage Manager	**Rosh Conn (any pronouns)**
Stage Manager & Operator [for Soho 2025]	**Daniel McVey (he/they)**

With thanks to:

Anthony Simpson-Pike, Charlie Josephine, Emma Frankland, Yasser Zadeh, Clapham Omnibus, Ugly Duck & Deen Atger, The Queer House, Cecil Fenn, LCY, Rob Hall, Cara V, Alex Brenner, Erica Belton, Finn Crawley, Jackson Dean, Ben Atterbury & Tan Follet & the whole team at Bristol Old Vic, Arts Council England, Stage One, Nick Coupe & Hat Trick Productions, Tom de Keyser, Kevin Kane.

Pete MacHale (he/him)
Playwright & Performer

Pete MacHale is a transmasculine actor and writer from Bristol. He trained at Arts University Bournemouth. Pete's writing credits include WhatsOnStage Award-nominated *Dear Young Monster* (Bristol Old Vic; Soho Theatre); *Born Actor* (Montez Press); *Shake My Bones* (as part of the Royal Court's Queer writers group); and *Still Here* created with Arts University Bournemouth. He is currently developing a number of projects for both stage and screen. Selected acting credits include *Let The Right One In* (Royal Exchange Theatre); *Dear Elizabeth* (Gate Theatre); *Doctor Who* (BBC); *Choose or Die* (Cursor Films/Netflix); *Gangs of London* (Sky Atlantic), and *Nânt* (Ffilm Cymru, Welsh BAFTA nominee). His most recent short, *Purebred*, is one of five shorts to have been nominated for Screen Ireland's Emerging Directors Awards 2025.

Sammy J Glover (they/them)
Director & Dramaturg

Sammy is a director and dramaturg who focuses on new writing, adaptations, and devised work with performer-creators. They are interested in telling queer stories and working with young people to create plays rooted in their communities. Recent productions include the sell-out devised show *The Last Show Before We Die* (Roundabout, Edinburgh Festival; The Yard Theatre, London; Bristol Old Vic; the Queer Performance Festival Vienna), and *Dear Young Monster*, the debut play by Pete MacHale (Bristol Old Vic; Soho Theatre).

They were associate director on Alex Zeldin's *The Other Place* at the National Theatre, and assisted Rebecca Frecknall on her production of *The Duchess of Malfi* at the Almeida Theatre. They were formerly Associate Director of Targeted Work at the Lyric Hammersmith, Resident Director at The Almeida Theatre, and Associate Director at The Big House, and they work as a Mentor Director for the National Theatre Connections programme each year. Sammy was also involved in creating the International Bruntwood Playwriting Reader Training, the first unconscious-bias reader training for playwriting prizes of its kind.

Jess Donn (he/they)
Producer

Jess is an independent producer based in Manchester. In 2025, he founded Just Something Different, a new production company to create and champion bold Queer work.

Key work that Jess has produced includes: *Dear Young Monster* ['Truly important', Bristol 24/7] (Bristol Old Vic; Soho Theatre); *Coming Out Of My Cage* (*And I've Been Doing Just Fine*) ['Irresistibly gleeful', The Guardian; 'A must-see', The Independent] (Shepard Tone Theatre); *Delicious Fruit* ['Marvellously multi-faceted', The Scotsman] (Plaster Cast Theatre).

Jess trained on the Stage One Regional Producer Placement with Mercury Theatre Colchester, and has continued to be supported by the Stage One Bursary.

Jess currently also holds Associate Producer positions at award-winning companies

Bechdel Theatre, Shepard Tone and Plaster Cast Theatre. He is a fundraiser, workshop facilitator, and access worker for neurodiverse artists. Throughout all of these endeavours, they continue to make work that is ambitious, genuine and hopeful.

Cara Evans (they/she)
Designer

Cara Evans is a London Based performance designer. Cara graduated in Design for Stage from the Royal Central School of Speech and Drama and was a reader at the Royal Court Theatre, London.

Theatre includes: as Designer or Co-Designer, *Feral Monster* (National Theatre Wales); *Sleepova* (Bush Theatre); *Dear Young Monster* (Bristol Old Vic; Soho Theatre); *The Living Newspaper*, *Queer Upstairs* (Royal Court); *Ugly Sisters* (New Diorama); *Wish You Were Here* (Gate Theatre); *Get Dressed!* (Unicorn); Statues (Bush Theatre); *Body Show* (Soho Theatre); *Sylvia* (English Theatre Frankfurt); *It's a Motherf**king Pleasure* (National Tour); *Millennium Girls* (Brixton House); *The Maladies* (Kiln Theatre); *Sirens* (Mercury Colchester); *SK Shlomo: Breathe* (Royal Albert Hall); *F**king Men* (Waterloo East); *The Beach House* (Park Theatre); *GRILLS* (Camden People's Theatre); *Love Bomb* (National Youth Theatre); *Baba Joon* (Swansea Grand Studio); *Bright Half Life* (King's Head); *The Misandrist* (Arcola); *Instructions for A Teenage Armageddon* (Southwark Playhouse). As Associate Designer for Chloe Lamford, *Teenage Dick* (Donmar School's Tour).

Hugo Dodsworth (he/him)
Lighting Designer

Hugo is a Performance Designer working across disciplines of set, lighting, and video design. He trained at Bristol Old Vic Theatre School.

Previous work includes *Dear Annie, I Hate You* (Riverside Studios; Pleasance Courtyard); *Henry V*, *Catastrophe Bay*, *Loam*, *Babytales* (Bristol Old Vic); *Sensory Cinders* (Soho Place); *Mariupol*, *Not the End of the World* (Cockpit Theatre); *The White Devil*, *Machinal*, *Mother Courage* (Royal Central School of Speech and Drama); *Angels in America*, *Balm in Gilead*, *The Cherry Orchard* (Tobacco Factory Theatres); *The Crucible* (the egg, Theatre Royal Bath); *The Last One* (Arcola).

Roly Botha (they/them)
Composer/Sound Designer

Roly is a theatremaker, composer, sound designer and performer, and an Associate Artist of The PappyShow.

Theatre includes: *Uncanny: Fear Of The Dark* (Tour); *Letters From Max* (Hampstead); *Playfight* (Soho; Bristol Old Vic; Roundabout); *Tambo & Bones* [additional music] (Theatre Royal Stratford East; Tour); *The Jungle Book* (Theatre By The Lake); *Shut Up I'm Dreaming* (National Theatre; Tour); *Dear Young Monster* (Soho; Bristol Old Vic); *Gunter* (Royal Court); *Truth & Tails* (Chichester Festival Theatre); *The Ultimate Pickle*, *A Sudden Violent Burst of Rain*, *Half Empty Glasses* (Paines Plough); *Orlando* (Jermyn Street); *Coming To England* (Birmingham Rep); *BOYS* (Barbican; Southbank Centre; tour); *WILD* (Unicorn); *Blowhole* (Soho Theatre); *Milk &*

Gall (Theatre503); *How To Fight Loneliness*, *Hir*, *Warheads* (Park Theatre) and *Brother* (Southwark Playhouse).

As music producer/orchestrator includes: *Diary Of A Gay Disaster* (Underbelly; Arcola, WhatsOnStage award for Best Studio Production)

As associate sound designer includes: *4:48 Psychosis* (Royal Court; RSC); *ECHO* (Royal Court; World Tour); *Cinderella* (Theatre Royal Stratford East)

Dee Dixon (she/her)
Video Designer

Dee Dixon is an audiovisual artist based in Manchester. Selected works include: *Toxic* (for Dibby Theatre National Tour inc Curve Theatre Leicester, The Lowry, Sheffield Theatres, Mercury Theatre Colchester); *Dear Young Monster* (Bristol Old Vic; Soho Theatre); *Delicious Fruit & Sound Cistem* (for Plaster Cast Theatre, Pleasance Theatre Edinburgh Fringe). She was also previously the VJ for the Marcus Intalex Music foundation's WK::END Festival, which saw her performing alongside artists Floating Points and Fabio as well being the visual designer for Ladymuck Theatre's The Amygdala and A/V designer for George Miaris' *The Way i See It*.

Conor Divers (he/him)
Associate Lighting Designer
[for Soho Theatre 2025]

Connor Divers is a Cumbrian lighting designer based in London. Design credits include *Magdalena, Woman of Joy* (Playhouse East, London); *Places I Never Think About* (The Omnibus); *The Tempest: This Island* (The Cockpit, London); *Broken* (Riverside Studios,

London); *Millennial Pink* (HOME, Manchester); *The Taming of Kate* (Teatro Blu, Milan). Upcoming: *Good Girls Don't Go To Hell* (The Divine Drag Bar, London), and *Moon River* (The Nest, Chichester Festival Theatre).

Katy Hoste (she/her)
Associate Designer
[for Bristol Old Vic 2024]

Katy Hoste is a freelance theatre designer/maker and painter dressed up as one person. Since training in Stage Design at the Royal Central School of Speech and Drama, she can usually be found telling stories in strange places. Katy's work focuses on set/costume and puppet design for theatre and live performance. She works in theatre, circus, and events across the country.

Loe D'Arcy (they/them)
Movement Director

Loe is a dancer and movement practitioner working across education, community and theatre settings. Recently in receipt of Arts Council England's DYCP fund, they have been training with artists and organisations including Clean Break, John Wright, and Ellen Lauren. Loe's approach is grounded in bodily listening as a tool for connection, expression, and agency within theatrical storytelling.

mandla (no pronouns)
Dramaturg
[for Bristol Old Vic 2024]

mandla is a Zimbabwean-born agender and queer writer and performer whose work often draws on the artist's intersectional existence. Using words as a medium, the artist is heavily concerned with communicating the many sensations associated with being a person. mandla's work takes many forms including: poetry, theatre, dramaturgy (*Dear Young Monster*, *Ladyfriends*, *Eurydice had been loved*), film, workshop facilitation, event production/programming and cabaret - where mandla can be found performing as a cow, moo. mandla has been commissioned by or produced work with Switchflicker Productions, Black Gold Arts, Contact Theatre, Journeys Festival, Royal Exchange Theatre, Royal Court Theatre, Bolton Octagon, Art With Heart, Fringe of Colour, Marlborough Theatre, Gay Times, BFI, Harry Clayton-Wright, Good Chance Theatre, Voices Weaving, and Rhubaba Gallery to name not all but a few.

Pansy Studios
Marketing/PR Lead

Pansy Studios is a queer-led, multidisciplinary marketing and creative studio built on strategic thinking, unapologetic creativity, and nurturing community, founded by author & strategist Ellen Jones. They specialise in helping brands, organisations, charities, and creatives cut through the noise with marketing, digital, and social strategies that are thoughtful, bold, and built to last. Pansy Studios runs the largest directory of LGBTQ+ freelance talent in the world, connecting brands with a global network of queer creatives and ensuring LGBTQ+ people get paid.

Rosh Conn (any pronouns)
Technical Stage Manager

Since graduating from BA Professional Production Skills at Guilford School of Acting in 2014, Rosh has made a name for herself working on hundreds of Fringe shows. She has managed the technical and stage components of events big and small UK wide – including being Deputy Head of Stage at VAULT Festival. You may recognise her from the role of 'Janitor With The Rhinestoned Bum' from Shotgun Carousel's *The Grotteaux*.

Daniel McVey (he/they)
Stage Manager & Operator
[for Soho 2025]

Daniel McVey is a Nottingham based Stage Manager who has worked on a number of national tours and regional productions including (*the*) *Woman* (New Perspectives Theatre); *Outlawed* (Nonsuch Studios); *The Beekeeper of Aleppo* (Nottingham Playhouse; Liverpool Playhouse; UK Productions); *The Trials* (Nottingham Playhouse); *Chaos Casino* (Bridie Squires) and many more. Daniel is also a Writer, Director and Theatre Maker and was a 2024/25 New Associate for New Perspectives. Their latest play *Gnaw* has had performances in 2024 at Nottingham Playhouse's Amplify Festival and the University of Nottingham. His script *Richard of York* was a top 10 finalist in the Carlo Annoni International Playwriting Award 2024.

Just Something Different is a production company creating spaces where Trans and Queer narratives can empower, thrive and inspire audiences and artists alike.

Our producing process centres around joy, changing the narrative around Queer work while leaving the audience with an action to take. Collaborating closely with artists to create bold, unconventional work that keeps audiences involved, we bring ideas to life and create live moments that fizz.

Led by award-winning producer Jess Donn, we're always looking to take visionary ideas and make them into reality, experimenting with theatre to create something new, something bold... just something different than what has come before.

We help artists to tell their stories with certainty, with the hope we can change the narrative of Trans and Queer work while keeping our audiences meaningfully engaged. We look for work that uses art as a tool for dialogue, hope and sparking action. Where our audiences are an inherent part of the conversation and valued for their time and attention.

The result? We aim for you to leave our productions with fire in your belly and momentum to go out in the world and make change.

Ready to build a more hopeful future?

DEAR YOUNG MONSTER

Pete MacHale

To Mum, for putting up with all of it.
Thank you.
Love you.

A Letter to Readers

Dear Young Monster is a show that has been in the making since 2018, born initially from a need to try and communicate the lived experiences of a young trans person growing up in the world around us. The original version shared seven years ago was short and a bit clumsy, but there was something sort of weird and alive at the heart of it that needed to be developed.

The experience of taking that initial seed and bringing this show to life with a team of incredible trans and queer creatives has affirmed that, like anyone else's, trans narratives deserve the time, space and support to be as nuanced and messy as they need to be. The extraordinary response to the show has taught us that in the UK today, stories like this are both urgent and necessary.

At the end of 2024, people under the age of eighteen questioning their gender identity in the UK were stripped of their access to healthcare with an indefinite ban on puberty blockers. In April 2025, the UK Supreme Court ruled that the definitions of man and woman were defined by biological sex only. Following this, the Equality and Human Rights Commission introduced interim guidance that makes it harder to live freely as a trans person. Every day, it becomes harder for trans people, especially trans kids, to be seen, to be respected, and to be safe.

We are not so naive as to believe one play can fix all this, but it is our sincere hope that in the face of such injustices against the trans community, *Dear Young Monster* becomes not just a coming-of-age story, but an act of resistance. We do not ask for your pity – we demand your recognition. We ask you to sit with us, to listen and look for yourself, trans or cis, in this journey. There is joy, power and beauty in finding yourself, whatever that looks like.

To trans people navigating this world with us: we honour you.

To those actively fighting for trans rights: we thank you.

With rage and hope,
Pete MacHale and Sammy J Glover

July 2025

Dear Young Monster was first performed at the Bristol Old Vic on 22 February 2024. The cast was as follows:

PERFORMER   Pete MacHale (he/him)

Director & Dramaturg   Sammy J Glover (they/them)
Producer   Jess Donn (he/they)
Designer   Cara Evans (they/she)
Lighting Designer   Hugo Dodsworth (he/him)
Composer/Sound Designer   Roly Botha (they/them)
Video Designer   Dee Dixon (she/her)
Associate Designer   Katy Hoste (she/her)
Movement Director   Loe D'Arcy (they/them)
Dramaturg   mandla (no pronouns)
Technical Stage Manager   Rosh Conn (any pronouns)

Notes on the Text

The play is performed as a monologue, spoken by one character. He acts as narrator, as himself within scenes, and voices the other characters he speaks to throughout.

Dialogue he speaks as other characters is shown 'in quotation marks like this', the character speaking should be clear from context.

The character telling the story is a transgender man, he should be played by an actor whose own identity aligns with/is adjacent to/encompasses that.

This text went to press before the end of rehearsals and so may differ slightly from the play as performed.

A projection: An older man in a suit and bow tie sweeps a velvet curtain aside and steps through into the centre of the image. It's the warning that plays at the beginning of Frankenstein, *1931. He tells the audience that the film studio felt it would be unkind to subject them to such a film without a friendly disclaimer. He explains that the feature is an exceptionally strange tale, that might thrill, shock, and even horrify. But he has warned you.*

The projection cuts out, and the show begins.

One

It's like being kept in a coffin.

Buried deep in the earth.

Six feet under and boxed in on all sides.

Your body doesn't fit.

You squirm and wriggle but the more you struggle the more you feel the walls closing in.

So you start to scratch. With your arm bent backwards and wrapped around your neck you stretch your finger out and painstakingly pull your nail against the wood.

Reeeeeetch.

Reeeeeeeeeeeettcchhh.

Scratch, scratch, scratch, shuffle, shift, nails split, splinters chew into the meat, harder, scratch harder, faster, deeper, you bang, you scream, you jerk and thrash until the wood, soggy, rotted, starts to give way and now you're in the dirt.

You push, burrow, onward, upward, slow, determined, out out out.

It fills your mouth, your ears, all your senses smeared with mud but you push and push and suddenly, somewhere bright and clean your bloody, messy, broken fingernails punch through the floor of a doctor's office!

'Good afternoon. So, how can I help you today?'

You heave yourself out of the ground and you sit in a chair.

'I see. And how was it? Being entombed?'

The doctor stares at you expectantly as your brain drips out of your ear. You've only screamed for years now. You try to make the shapes, to tell him what it was like deep under the earth. But when you open your mouth, mud, worms, and teeth fall out.

'Interesting, and if it's okay to ask, not offensive to ask, how did you survive down there? What did you do to pass the time, and sorry this is on the form, did you drink? Smoke? Do drugs? Did you try to kill yourself?'

No.

Yes.

I'm only seventeen.

'That's true… Right. Brilliant, thank you for sharing all of that, I'm glad you felt empowered to come and talk to me. I think let's give it a bit more time, and if you're sure we can start making the appropriate calls.'

No, but I didn't mean –

'Thank you.'

So you wait.

And you wait some more.

And you turn eighteen.

And you wait, and you wait and you start uni and you try really hard but you're putrid and rotting and falling apart and you can't really talk to anyone still so you drop out and you wait and wait (et cetera) and then.

FINALLY.

They decide you can live.

So here we are. A time, a place, a vial of liquid. The *golden elixir of life.*

The sun is almost down and its reaching rays push shadows between houses into the cobbled road.

I plaster myself to the dark side of the street, using the shadow as cover from watching eyes wandering home on the opposite pavement.

The road I arrive at seems normal, familiar even, but the building I want leans back heavily. Older, more tired. And as I get to the end of the driveway, the gates hang open slack-jawed to welcome me in.

The waiting room is empty and I almost have a second to catch my breath when I notice a *figure filling the doorway.*

'Here for the six p.m.?'

I swallow thickly and a river of sweat drenches my back.

He nods.

'Great. Follow me.'

We walk down a long corridor, turn left and right and back on ourselves until we're deep in the guts of the building. He holds a door open. I step inside…

AND SUDDENLY I'm bent awkwardly over a cold medical table, skin bare and flushed with panic! I crane my neck to try and see over my shoulder but all I glimpse is a long point, raised high before I feel a SPIKE, swift and sharp… the world goes black.

He contorts wildly and collapses in a broken heap on the floor. He waits. He waits. He waits… Until he lifts his head and grins cheekily at the audience.

I just had my first testosterone injection!

It feels… it feels fucking amazing.

You wait so long for this moment.

The waiting feels like a lifetime, like it goes on forever and ever and ever past how long you can even imagine, and I didn't even wait that long. Compared to others.

After all that it does feel slightly anticlimactic to pass out on your, quite fit, nurse when he stabs you in the bum. Low blood pressure. Still.

When I walk back home, back through the *cobbles* and *looming houses*, the darkness seems to soften it all a bit.

It feels safe to stop and stand there for a moment.

I picture the chemical reactions inside me. $C19H28O2$.

The liquid in the needle was thick and gluey and I can imagine it coating the inside of my veins. Soaking the strings of my muscles. Oil on water, T on blood.

The first thing I do when I get home from the GP is race upstairs to the bathroom to stare at my own face for probably, roughly, maybe, about an hour.

Other than a miraculous wisp of bumfluff I'm not really sure what I expect to see.

Just something different?

And I know, obviously, nothing's actually changed. Yet.

But I'm waiting to finally feel the spark of something. A tingle, a zap, the fizz of something between my fingers and down my spine as my body transforms.

I can't wait till hair crawls up my belly.

I can't wait till my piss smells different. I read that that happens online. Testosterone changes the smell of your sweat and piss.

But, obviously, there's no difference, yet. Obviously. Obviously.

Still.

Two

The next day nothing really changes.

And the next day, nothing really changes.

And then the next day, and the next day, and the next week.

And *then* I get a cough, and my voice gets deeper and I'm like *FUCKING YES*, but then the cough goes, and the deep voice goes with it, so maybe not fucking finally after all.

Basically the only real difference after a month is I have spots now.

'It's genetics', 'it's different for everyone, just like normal puberty!' Yeah I know, but come on.

Another month whizzes by and I might as well have not suffered through the bum trauma.

I do feel like something must be changing, but I'm worried it's all in my head because it's not exactly standard puberty fare.

My skin feels a little too tight, my energy feels a little too up, I'm always a little too warm now. Sweaty. And I'm hungry, hungry all the time, ever since I started my appetite is monstrous –

'ARE YOU COMING BACK IN OR NOT?'

My best friend Mia. She's sitting cross-legged on her bed waiting for me, film still paused on the TV on her desk. She asks slightly tentatively,

'Gone a while, you alright?'

I throw myself onto the floor, same spot as I always sit, same spot as I sat the first time I ever came to her house five years ago. Where she pulled some vintage vinyl out from under her bed and proudly whispered to me that she stole it, and she'd never shown anyone else, and I realised she was basically the coolest person I'd ever met.

Yeah fine, had a spot. Come on, press play.

He and Mia sit and watch The Thing. *He quietly fills in the audience as they watch, talking aside to them. Something is bothering him, making him fidgety, and uncomfortable.*

On the TV a man's stomach rips open into a fanged mouth. The skin-teeth clamp on to the arms of the man who's trying to save him. Crunches through them.

I cringe. Mia laughs.

Mia loves gore, but hates it, 'loves to hate it' kind of thing.

Skin splits, blood spurts and the second man drops dead on the floor as a slimy chimera explodes from the first guy's shredded stomach cavity.

Mia triumphantly announces 'That's fucking gross.'

We've been going backwards through the decades all summer, since she came home from uni.

Started with a load of A24, then the 2000s, lots of J-horror – *The Ring*, the original proper one from ninety-eight; then the actual nineties, mostly teen slashers; and now we're working through eighties classics together.

The Thing on TV roars and twitches its juddering spidery appendages, greasy and bug-eyed – then mid-screech the monster freezes.

Mia has paused the film. She's pointing the remote at me accusingly.

'What's going on, you're being weird.'

I'm not being weird.

'Um. You are.'

The dripping pink monster stares down at us, teeth jutting, tongue lolling. Looks like a big veiny dick with a face.

It's just a bit gross.

'It's cool, we like this stuff?'

You do.

…

She doesn't move. Crosses her arms. I try to reach for the remote and she holds it over my head. I get up, she stands up on the bed, I jump, she snatches it out of reach again.

Give it.

'What's wrong?'

Just give it.

'Tell me.'

It's nothing

'It's not.'

Mia, can we just watch the STUPID FILM!

...

Her eyes widen for a second, and then she drops back onto the bed. Her face to the floor. She holds out the remote. I look at it dangling between us.

It used to be really rare to see Mia facing down, she's such an upward person. But I feel like I've been seeing it more and more lately.

We never used to argue but this summer it's like she's been half here, like she's sad to be back. Sad to be where I am.

...

Sorry I'm just, it's just, you're leaving. I'm going to be stuck here alone. Again.

I'll have no one to watch stupid films with or tell me what's changing and get excited when my voice breaks and even now it's like you don't even get it so I don't know why I'm so bothered about you going.

She snaps up, suddenly annoyed.

'That's not fair. What do you mean I don't get it?'

I don't know you just don't, you can't, like you literally just called me weird –

'Well yeah. You're weird.

Beat.

Can you try and explain?'

...I just want to watch this film. With you. Before you go. Even though it's making me feel sick. Even though it's making my skin crawl because I'm warm all over all the time and I feel uncomfortable and prickly and I wake up sweating and just then, with all the blood and...

'Maybe you're going through menopause?'

His jaw drops. For a moment he's fuming, but then it sinks in.

Oh my god, maybe I'm going through menopause.

Mia bursts out laughing again.

'OH MY GOD YOU'RE MY NAN.'

And I try not to laugh... but it makes me laugh, 'cause Mia always makes me laugh. And she laughs harder, and falls off the bed so I laugh harder too.

She manages to catch her breath long enough to say:

'So wait, does that mean your period has stopped?'

Uh... maybe? It's definitely late.

'Mate! That's massive! First change on T, right?'

I guess, yeah.

Suddenly she grabs my head. Vice-grip holds me still and eyes searching my face until they start to bug out of her head like the Thing on the TV.

What are you doing?

'Before and after pic. This is the before, and when I get back home for Christmas holidays you'll be the after. I bet you're gonna be like, twice the size. With a fuckin' beard, or something.'

I won't be, obviously.

But she grins up at me and her teeth are small and sweet in her mouth, like Tic Tacs.

I'm gonna miss you loads.

'Yeah I'm not dying, you idiot. You can ring me if you miss me.'

Three

I post photos online.

On a trans support forum. Cringe.

I ask:

Hey everyone, been on T for a few months now. Not sure im seein much change lol, do u think i pass? Pic in comments.

I get replies:

Yes definitely, I am thirty-four bro, not on hormones u look more male than me!

One hundred per cent looking good bro.

Very handsome lad, you pass to me mate.

Lots of 'bro'. I don't think I can trust someone who calls me 'bro'.

It's a bit forced. Like they're trying to prove something. Not sure if it's for me or for themselves.

A bit like how I remember boys being in Year Eight. Me and Mia would watch them do press-ups in the field at lunch while they cheered each other on. Go on lad! Go on bro! Don't be gay!

I'm not sure if I'm gay. Kind of hard to know who you want to be close to if you're not ready for anyone to be close to you. Not that that mattered to them, I'd always catch them checking that people were still watching.

I'm not sure how I'm supposed to feel if nothing's changed yet.

I feel like I actually felt better on the day I was getting my injection ten minutes before my injection than now that I've actually had my injection.

Because then at least it wasn't like I had any expectations.

At least before when I went to the shop and the shop man goes 'Hello madam' I could think well yeah, of course, once I start my injections *that won't happen*! But now I've had my second injection, and 'Hello madam' in the shop feels like a kick in the teeth instead of a punch in the gut.

Every single day I check for some sign of masculinisation.

A slowly squaring jawline perhaps? Something different about my nose?

Thicker… eyebrows?

That spark I thought I'd feel, it doesn't happen.

A strange face stares back at me from the mirror. Me, but not me, but not the right not-me. I wait for it to wink.

My mum says it must be working because I'm starting to look like my uncle Joe. Which is weird cause he's my step-uncle, but she's trying to be nice.

She says:

'Why don't you get out and about, get some fresh air, socialising?'

Mia's gone back for second year.

'Why don't you pop down the pub, maybe have a pint with some of *the other lads.*'

I leave. To get her to drop it. I know she means well but…

Outside, playing, is the little girl who lives over the road and three doors down.

She has a little brown bob and she seems to have an endless supply of those old-school T-shirts that have a little stuffed

lizard sewn onto the shoulder because she's wearing them
whenever I see her. Today the lizard is yellow.

She sees me coming out of my house and raises her hand to
wave… but then she stops.

He realises something.

She doesn't recognise me.

He grins.

Because I look different.

*He waves excitedly back to the little girl, until her mum's voice
sharply cuts in.*

'Who are you waving to?'

'Next-door lady!'

He drops his arm defeatedly.

You can trust kids, they don't have any agenda, nothing to
prove.

Four

He paces his bedroom as he leaves Mia a voice note.

Hey mate, how are you, how's it all going, how's second year
going? Good, good?

This is my voice, four months on T! Lol.

Missing you loads. Not really much to do with you away.

Is the flat better yet? Have you got the microwave sorted? Can't
believe she just stuck the takeout thing in the microwave, that's
just, can't even believe someone would do that!

Watched *Texas Chainsaw Massacre* the other day, you made
it sound sick, felt like I was missing out so… Thought it was

pretty good! Kind of sad though, I think, at the end? But big final-girl vibes, loved that.

I've got my next appointment with the gender clinic next week so I had to have my blood taken yesterday. Saved you some, obviously! They said if they're happy with my testosterone levels, like normal boy-levels, not that it should make a difference, then I *finally* get to start talking about surgery, maybe, which is sick. Next summer could be my first topless summer!

I was thinking maybe we could plan going swimming. I know it's ages away but you know. I don't think I'd be ready for the beach or a public pool so we could see if there's some other place.

Not much else has changed I don't think. Or well, Mum took down that ugly painting in the hallway.

Sounds like you were having a really good time the other day though! What were you doing, like two messages up? When that boy was shouting in the background? Who is he? Was it like a party or something?

Would be cool to maybe ring this weekend? Talk about *Texas Chainsaw*? I'll probably be around whatever.

Five

THE MONSTER IS LOOSE!!!

'SPOOKY OCTOBER FRIDAY FRIGHT NIGHTS NINE POUNDS.'

A huge gaunt face with heavy-set eyes stares down at me from the poster outside the cinema.

Mia would hate this.

We do spooky October every year but we always miss the last one 'cause she says 'black-and-white films are boring'.

But Mia's not here.

I go inside and head to the ticket counter. It feels a bit exciting to say '*one* please'.

'Can I see some ID?'

ID, the nemesis of transexuals.

I've been meaning to change it, but it's eighty quid for a new passport and you can't change the gender marker until you get a letter from your doctor which you have to request through your GP and it feels sort of silly to send in a photo when there's a chance my face will just look different again another two months down the line and – I haven't sorted it yet.

I hand it over.

The cashier flips it open, looks between me and the beaming gap-toothed girl on the page.

Me. Little girl. Me.

I try a smile, try to make us match a bit more.

She sort of wrinkles her nose, sighs, snaps my passport shut.

'Nine pounds.'

No going back now.

I step alone into the dark cavern of the screening room.

There's no one else really here, which is… sort of nice.

I deflate into the patchy velvet seat and the *click*-whirrrrrr of the film reel starts in my ears.

A scene from Frankenstein*.*

Elizabeth is in her wedding dress, sitting in her bedroom. The monster climbs through the window as she paces the floor, and stalks toward her. She turns and sees the monster, screams, and it growls back, an oddly comical 'rowwarr.'

He watches the clip transfixed.

He raises his hands, wiggling his fingers.

I can feel it.

It's that feeling I've been waiting for. The fizzing in my fingers.

A jolt, a shock, a humming just beneath my skin, something surging through my veins, my body awakening, buzzing to life finally, FINALLY.

Something about the monster, the way he moves through the world, the way others move around him.

The outsider. The man-made man. A cruel joke the way he's almost the same but not quite right.

I could feel the monster's big, dead, sad eyes looking down from the screen, right at me.

…

I head home.

But as I go I keep thinking about the monster.

My legs stiffen and my shoulders square.

My arms start to swing, pendulums, stiff but free, and my feet land heavier and heavier as I feel myself falling into the monster's massive body.

Bolts screw into my neck and each lumbering step I take shocks me, jump-starts me, tops me up and now I'm pumped, like, I feel GOOD!

I want to go somewhere, I want to do something, for the first time in fucking ages!

I see the light of a building back down the hill, so I lurch towards it.

The monster's uneven legs march me, wonky, up to the pub.

His big rotting hand reaches and slumps against the door, and he leans my weight into it, pushing it open, grinding on its hinges.

My head lolls and the monster's groan gurgles in my belly, crawls its way up my throat.

'UURRrgghHHHH –'

Echoing out of my hanging mouth –

'RRGGGUHUHHGHHHHHH'

I lift my head, eyes wide and rolling and –

'RRRRRHHHH –'

Stop.

The entire pub has stopped.

Staring at me.

What the fuck am I doing?

The eyes peel away. The Friday-night noise starts to burble up again. I make a beeline for the bar. I mumble my way through ordering a pint and take it outside to sit, alone, on the wooden picnic bench.

Inside the pub was a warm lively orange, but out here it's a bit grey and cold.

I hear an explosion of laughter, and I turn to look through the window. Through the screen of the frost-tinted glass. I watch unfamiliar rituals inside.

It's fascinating.

At one table a man rolls cigarette after cigarette, passing each to a waiting friend. His rolling is practised and perfected, they seem to know exactly when to hold out a hand without ever looking down.

At the bar, three older men sit in a line, separate and wordless. One raises his pint and takes a gulp, then the next lifts his, and the next lifts his. A dance in canon.

Another group of men stand in a circle, one has his arm around his girlfriend's waist, holding her tight against him. They swing their drinks high above their heads and clang them together.

There's a strange rhythm to it all. A pulse I don't quite have yet.

I can't stop watching.

Their movements get looser as the drinks pour faster. The beat speeds up and syncopates, they unravel. Two men miss the timings, collide, and the drumming charges on as fists wrap into shirts and they swing each other out the doors.

A quick scuffle and some aborted punches are obscured by puffs of breath which hang as clouds in the night air. They come apart and for a moment are both bent double, winded, but then they straighten... And begin to laugh? Slap each other on the back. Their arms drop over one another's shoulders and they turn to head back inside.

As they walk past, one of them sees me.

I test out my newly witnessed knowledge, and raise my empty pint slightly.

He grins, and bobs his head. Then they disappear back into the belly of the beast, and I'm left outside.

Six

She's there again.

The little girl who lives over the road and three doors down.

She's playing on the low-rise wall between hers and the neighbours' front garden.

She sits, then she stands, then does a jump, sits back down. She goes 'lalalalala' to herself quietly.

I'm instantly petrified.

I'm tempted to curl back into the darkness of my hallway.

I'm tempted to slink back upstairs to bed.

Hiding from a little girl, 'cause she thinks I'm... Yeah.

Pathetic.

I actually cringe at the thought of myself. Top lip tightening upwards in disgust and tiny moustache hairs tickle my nose.

…Moustache… *MOUSTACHE HAIRS* TICKLE MY NOSE!

I spin to the mirror, tilt my head and flare my nostrils and I can almost see all the way up to my brain but there they are!

A scattering of hairs waving at me from my top lip!

They weren't there last night, were they? I swear they weren't, can't have been.

Maybe I missed them? Maybe they grew while I was sleeping? Who cares really?

Suddenly it's the easiest thing in the world to stride out the door and march over the road, ready to take on the mammoth task of correcting a six-year-old.

I'm going to tell her that *actually* I'm a boy – a man! I'm a man.

I'm about to clear my throat when I see the slightly ajar front door swings open and her mum appears.

Her mum looks him up and down.

'Inside now.'

Mum's thin-lipped and frowny.

She snaps her words and holds the door wide enough only for her daughter to fit through. Looks at me like I might drop onto all fours and give chase, like she needs to slam the door in a nick of time.

The girl looks to her mum, then to me.

'I said now.'

She hops down from the wall, twirling a garden flower, and toddles inside.

Just before her mum closes the door she hisses something. Maybe 'fffuck off' maybe 'fffreak'.

She narrows her eyes at me. Shakes her head. Slams the door.

Who the fuck does that? Who even shakes their head at people any more?

Okay I get it right, stranger danger, who's the weirdo at the front door?

Except I'm not!

They've seen me before, I've actually lived over the road from them for like four years and okay, yeah, this isn't Happy Families Cul-de-Sac, epicentre of street parties and local barbecues but it's not like I'm some creepy figure in a trench coat!

It's not like I'm some awful –

It's three fucking moustache hairs.

…

There's a scene in *Frankenstein* where the monster meets a little girl.

A clip from Frankenstein *plays. The monster meeting little Maria by the river. As it plays behind him, without him seeing, he describes it beat for beat.*

She's sat on a riverbank and she's picking flowers, dropping them into the river where they float. They look like little stars all around her, bobbing gently like a drifting sky.

The monster, he's been stumbling through the woods, he's been pulled and pushed and whipped and chained and he's killed, he's killed someone to escape, all he's known until now is violence.

He sees the little girl by the river.

And for the first time in the whole film she's gentle.

She doesn't shout or scream, she giggles and shows him how to play her game.

The monster bends his beaten body into the soft grass and for the first time in the film you understand that he was really born only a few days ago.

He's trying to learn life at hyperspeed, he's seeing half the dots and trying to connect them with no chance to practise, just be this, do this, feel this, know this.

She picks up a flower, throws it in the river and laughs.

He picks up a flower.

He throws it in the river.

She laughs.

He picks her up.

Throws her in the river.

Laughs.

Behind him, in the projection, Maria drowns.

He's just watching, and learning, and doing.

He's just trying to make her laugh.

Seven

He's manic, locked away in his bedroom. Everything is starting to get to him. He flits between confidently addressing the audience and leaving Mia a string of increasingly agitated voice notes.

Boris Karloff. That's the guy who played Frankenstein's monster. The guy under all the [make-up].

I've been looking him up. Online, read articles, watch interviews, rewatch the film and check in the mirror if my shoulders are any wider.

Hey Mia, how are you? You seen any good movies lately? I haven't really been watching anything… new. You still seeing radish guy? I miss you!

He was spotted by the director while having his lunch one day. He walked up to him and said, famously, 'your face has startling possibilities'.

Just me again! This is my voice, seven months on T! I grew some moustache hairs but uh, I've been shaving them off... just 'cause they look a bit pubey. Sent you a photo. Talk soon!

So Karloff was whisked away with a make-up artist to create the Monster behind closed doors! Two weeks it took, holed away.

Just me again, again! Probably starting to look a bit like that 'after' picture now. Sort of.

Two weeks! Two weeks to build a monster, two weeks sat in a make-up chair watching your face transform before your very eyes.

Heeeeeey Mia, did you watch that film I sent you?

TWO WEEKS! They took out Karloff's dentures to make his cheeks more hollow, pulled his mouth down with a wire and distended his head with rolls of cotton. They carved scars out of cloth and liquid collodion.

They said his eyes were too kind, so they drooped them down with mortician's wax.

Two weeks up in my room and all I've done is amass used cups.

...

Mia hasn't replied yet.

I think second year must just be really hard 'cause she didn't come back for the Christmas holiday in the end, either.

But on Christmas eve I got my mum to watch *How the Grinch Stole Christmas* with me. Boris Karloff narrates it, and voices the Grinch.

After it finished I went back upstairs to my room, and watched *Frankenstein* again. And again.

There's a story in one interview I watched, that the director came to approve the iconic Monster's make-up before it was revealed to the world.

He walked into the room and Karloff was sitting in the make-up chair waiting for him. His face all –

He pulls a Frankenstein's Monster face.

And he turned to the director and said:

In a lisp:

'I think this will be the most sensational thing ever seen on the silver screen.'

I LOVE IT!

There he is, this terrifying face, two-week face, wired, waxy, wonderful face and he christens it:

'Sensational.'

I love it.

A face so monstrous. A face no one could love.

But he did.

He called it sensational.

I love it. I love it. I love it.

Eight

'Hello, love, knock knock.'

My mum, standing, worrying the doorway.

Heya, you alright?

'Yeah, yeah. Just thought I'd pop up and see if you're alright?'

Yeah I'm alright.

'Yeah just because… Are you sure you're alright? Really? Feel like you've been very locked away up here? Haven't seen much of you lately.'

What's going on, Mum?

'No, no nothing. It's just… Well sorry. I picked up the post earlier and, sorry I know I shouldn't have opened it but it had… Your *old* name on it so I thought maybe you wouldn't want to, and…'

Is that letter for me? Is that from the gender clinic?

He snatches a letter out of his mum's hand. He excitedly opens and reads the letter, but as he does he visibly deflates.

We're very sorry… Delays in surgery referral… estimated another six-to-seven months.

'Sorry, love. I know you were excited for this… change. And now I don't, I don't want you to let this get to you too much. And I was thinking, and I'm sorry I know I shouldn't have, but when I was reading it downstairs I was thinking that maybe this is a chance to keep having a think about it all, you know? It's a really big decision. Irreversible if you change your mind. Irreparable, really.'

What do you mean?

'Just that I don't wonder if some more time would be a good thing? Just so you're definite.'

No, what do you mean by 'irreparable'?

Why would you say 'irreparable'? Do you think I'm breaking myself?

'You know I really support you, I really do. I just want to be sure. That you're ready.'

I get up. Make to leave but she's still standing in the doorway.

'Are you going to be alright?'

Yeah, Mum. Are you though? That seems to be more important.

She's still, but she sort of winces, like I see it in her eyes. For half a second I feel bad and then my brain whispers 'irreparable', and I shove past, barrel down the stairs and out the front door.

Six-to-seven months.

More months.

Could be longer.

My face feels hot and my hands clench and I feel tears prick behind my eyes for the first time in fucking ages.

Testosterone can sometimes stop you crying, but right now I feel like something inside me is leaking, something in the centre of me.

Something that was holding on to the hope that maybe soon this body might feel a little bit more like home. But now that hope has burst and it's seeping out, it's oozing out of me like pus.

More waiting.

I screw up my face, clench my eyes shut to try and stifle the tears. Try and stop the hope from escaping.

When I open them she's there again.

Door ajar, playing on the wall, flower in hand.

She's got this look on her face, startled, almost like fear, like she doesn't know what I am and for a second she looks thin-lipped, frowny, just like her mum.

So I make a face back.

He makes his monster face, but it's wrong. Twisted. Bigger, exaggerated, scary.

She drops the flower and runs inside.

Nine

I'm alone on the beach. I crack a can and take a long drink.

Drink and think.

Think about the little girl over the road. Next-door lady.

Drink.

Think about how Mia hasn't phoned me back in ages.

Drink.

Irreparable.

Drink.

Think about the monster.

I crack another can and I jar and sway like Karloff.

He reaches his hands out in front of him, mimicking a pose of the Monster. He makes the Frankenstein's Monster face again, laughs despite himself, drunkenly sways a little – then suddenly he stops.

Turn, look... Nothing.

He shakes it off.

He starts to dance.

It's a strange blend of a Frankenstein's Monster impression and drunken-dad dancing. He trips and twirls, losing himself to the freedom of the Monster, until he is just playing, running around the space with flashes and poses of a waltz, a wobbly bow, a flourish of arms.

The movement winds down until he is brought to near still, moving slowly and gently in a circle as if dancing with a phantom partner.

He turns out to the audience, and realises he is being watched. He flees.

Ten

Me and Mia are watching *Dracula* tonight!

Or watched. We made a plan to both watch it at the same time and live-text it to each other, then phone afterwards to debrief.

I like it. I did!

The lead actor is really good, the guy who plays Dracula.

He has this angular shadowy face, and he's the original 'Dracula voice', the one that everyone does when they're doing Dracula.

He's got really piercing eyes, intense eyes. They stand out through the black-and-white slashes of the film in a way that's quite… freaky.

It's a good film.

It's just…

Well it's not *Frankenstein*, is it!

'I haven't seen *Frankenstein*.'

What? Really? But I've told you about it loads. I thought you had watched it?

'Yeah, no, I know, I've got the voicenotes. I just, I haven't watched it.'

Oh. Okay. Well… what did you think then? Of *Dracula*?

'Yeah it was jokes, "Volves, cheeeeldrin of de naaight, I vant to sack your blaaaad".'

He makes a face.

Confession, I've seen *Dracula* before. I watched it a while ago but Mia wanted to watch it tonight, get on the 'old-school movie hype' with me, and it's been ages so, you know.

I looked up *Dracula* when I watched it, like I did *Frankenstein*. I looked up the actor who played him.

I say to Mia, you know, it's really interesting, he's really cool actually, Bela Lugosi.

'Who?'

Dracula.

He was this film actor in Hungary, so his accent, like the Dracula voice, it's not Transylvanian, it's Hungarian. He moved to America because of some political tension, but he wasn't as successful.

He struggled to find work, sort of 'cause of his accent, the fact he was foreign, different, you know. So he ended up working on stage playing... Dracula. That's how he got the part in the movie.

He'd be pacing the halls of the castle where they were filming, and reciting his lines, in his Hungarian accent, and all the American actors would make fun of him and say he 'really thought he was Dracula'.

So I think just maybe, it's a bit weird if you... do the voice.

'Uh. Yeah no, definitely.'

She seems a bit exasperated but the floodgates have opened now.

DID YOU KNOW, he was actually offered the role of the monster in *Frankenstein*, but he turned it down. Wouldn't have been the same. You should really watch it, you know. But maybe he should have taken the part.

He did work on other films after, I mean it made him famous. But he was the *Dracula* guy. He wanted to be a leading man but he was always pushed to play vampiric villains instead.

Apparently his career started to decline. He struggled with addiction and work dried up and eventually he moved to England, and went back to playing Dracula on stage.

I read somewhere that he was buried in his cape. Bela Lugosi was buried in his cape.

'That's really sad.'

What? Why is that sad?

'I don't know, it makes me sort of angry. Like, it sounds like he never escaped playing this character that he hated, and other people get to decide that the last thing he'll ever do is wear the costume of the thing he didn't want to be in his grave. Do you not think that's sad?'

I don't think he hated Dracula. His wife and daughter said it's what he would have wanted.

It's a great film. He'll be remembered forever.

'Yeah, as Dracula, not as… Well there you go. I can't even remember his name.'

Well that's your fault, I can remember it. And anyway what's wrong with being remembered as Dracula? As a monster? Boris Karloff loved his monster. He said playing the monster changed his life, gave him his career, he said, 'I owe him everything.' He said, 'He's my dear old monster.'

'Who's Boris Karloff?

Boris Karloff!

'Oh wait, the Frankenstein?'

…Mia it's Frankenstein's monster, everyone knows that.

'Right. Look, mate, I have to go. I've got a load of coursework I have to do, and I need to sort this costume for a party… I do like, miss you though. Sorry I haven't been around, life is just, I don't know, a lot right now.'

I could come!

'What?'

To the party. I miss you, you miss me. I could visit! For the party.

'Are you sure?'

Yeah! Why not!

'It's just… Are you alright? To come and visit I mean.'

Definitely. It'll be great.

Eleven

Mia's flatmates are really sweet! She lives with two other girls called Sophia and Fizz. Yeah, *Fizz*?

Fizz let me in after I arrived off the coach and gave me a beer basically immediately. She's really small and has pigtails and a nose ring and tells me she's 'sort of studying textiles' which I didn't know you could do a degree in.

Sophia is quieter but in a cool laid-back kind of way. She doesn't talk as much but she *does* have tooth gems.

The other two point me down the hall to Mia's room and I start to get a little nervous because when she texted me her address it was a bit blunt, but when she opens the door she looks genuinely relieved that I managed to arrive in one piece and gives me a quick hug.

She begins to show me around, she shows me her room and all the candles she's been hoarding arranged around a massive *Friday the 13th* poster. She shows me her non-stick frying pan and the tiny garden with one piece of patio furniture that she sits on when she goes for a ciggy. She shows me this weird old newspaper from 1983 that's stuck to their ceiling in the hallway, and then takes me into one of the other girls' bedrooms where Sophia pours each of us a glass of wine so we can start *pre-drinking.*

The girls put on music and sing along to songs I don't know while they get ready. They're going as the Powerpuff Girls. They're so cool.

Mia points at the Tesco bag I've been clutching since I arrived and asks,

'Go on then, what's in there?'

I start to edge toward the bathroom.

I say it's a surprise.

He sneaks off to the bathroom and takes out a costume. It's some kind of a suit. Something monstery, home-made, queer. He hangs it up in plain view and looks at it with reverence.

Projected behind him is the scene from Frankenstein, *the one we all know:*

The moment before they flip the switch. The doctor fusses about his creation, prone on the slab.

In the bathroom he begins to change his clothes.

The monster on the table rises up to the open hole in the roof to the storm raging over the castle. Sound kicks in. Electrical buzzing, thunder and whirring machines crunching and folding over each other getting louder and louder as the monster is struck by lightning. They bring the monster back down and the noise is almost deafening.

Frantic, excited, a little drunk... he begins to paint himself yellow.

Behind him the doctor fusses about the body, shrieking the famous line:

'It's alive... It's alive. IT'S ALIVE, IT'S ALIVE IT'S ALIVE IT'S ALIVE IT'S ALIVE – '

He stands and takes himself in, admires his handiwork.

Sensational.

'Uh... What are you?'

I'm the monster.

'What monster?'

...*The* Monster. Frankenstein's Monster.

'Isn't he supposed to be green?' chimes Fizz.

Well, yeah, no, actually. So *yes* the make-up, the monster was green, like green paint *but* in the book, originally the monster is described as being yellow, like yellowed dead flesh, but because the film is black-and-white having him be yellow wouldn't show up very well so they decided to paint him green for higher contrast BUT he was actually supposed to be yellow... like in the book.

Mia makes an expression that I don't recognise. Fizz stares into the middle distance and says, 'Ooooh... huh.'

I settle into a bean-bag chair and open another can.

I feel a little awkward sat doing nothing while they get ready, but Sophia catches my eye and says:

'Boys have it so easy.'

Which I think is kind of stupid 'cause I'm wearing like triple the amount of make-up, but the three girls laugh in agreement and I sort of glow inside.

On the bus to the party I sit next to Mia. We all chatter and joke and after a bit she hooks our arms together.

She tells the girls about how the first day we met I was wearing the girls' uniform trousers and she asked me why I looked uncomfortable and I didn't know how to explain myself so I just stood there with an expression like I was holding in a fart until she asked if I wanted to ditch and borrow her PE joggers, and that we've been best mates ever since.

Fizz goes 'That's soooo cute!' and Sophia says 'Madness.'

We all barrel off the bus and I grab Mia's hand, start running –

'YOU DON'T EVEN KNOW WHERE YOU'RE GOING!'

DON'T CARE! COME ON!

We skitter down the street, whooping and twirling, with Fizz and Sophia chasing behind. Mia takes the lead and drags me toward a house pulsing red, then blue, then red, then green –

The girls catch up and we each take another can from the Tesco bag we brought and make our way into the living room.

The music is… shit, but it's loud and energetic and Fizz manoeuvres me toward a group of other people who all light up at our arrival.

The girls seem to know everyone we bump into and at first I feel a little outside of it all, but with each drink introductions get easier. I start to think it's kind of nice being the new guy. I'm just Mia's boy mate from home. The drinks keep coming and everything starts to swirl together.

We've got this little group, Me and Mia, Fizz and Sophia, everyone we've collected. We swing out drinks up into the air, above our heads and screech when vodka and Coke and cider rains down onto us all and I feel... I FEEL....

A joyful monstrous cry.

I pull Mia into the centre, I spin, swing her around, let her go –

He dances harder, bigger, taking up more space.

I see Fizz, grab her, lock our hands and hold them high in the air –

'Ow, stop!'

Loop down, wrap around, hold her tight against me –

'I said STOP!'

She stamps on my foot, jab in the chest, back in the middle, back to the dance, back to the, someone pulling, get off me, want to, need to, GET OFF, FUCK OFF –

He explodes; aggressive, unrestrained, monstrous.

GET YOUR FUCKING HANDS OFF ME.

The party stops dead around him. Everyone is staring. Everyone's uncomfortable. He has crossed a line.

...

Outside it's fucking freezing, and it smells like foxshit.

'What the fuck is your problem?'

What?

'What were you doing in there? Those are my mates, you know.'

Mia's eyes dart around, she seems to be vibrating a little.

I don't understand what I did wrong.

'Fizz is really upset. She said doesn't feel comfortable with you staying at ours.'

But my coach back isn't till twelve.

'Well I don't know! I don't know what the fuck to do, everyone's really upset.'

Why?

'Because you're being weird.'

Right. Right, okay. I'm weird.

'No, don't do that. Don't fucking act like you knew this was going to happen.'

You're the one who called me weird, you just said –

'Because you're being fucking weird! 'Cause you grabbed my mate round the neck and you *hurt her*. Look, it's been ages since we got to spend some time together and it's genuinely really cool to see you and I get it you've had a hard time but this isn't about you being – different, or awkward or trans.

Here you're just a drunk guy who grabbed a girl at a party and screamed in someone's face. That's not okay. Doesn't matter how hard you have it.'

Sorry.

'Just go inside. Let me finish my fag.'

…

It's easy to find the toilet. I go back the way we came in, wander up the stairs.

The door is shut so I wait.

Group of guys are hanging about on the landing. One of them, face painted like a cheetah, keeps looking back at me. I look down at the floor to avoid his glances but I don't have to wait long. Someone blunders out, swinging the door wide, I slip in and quickly pull it shut.

The party is suddenly muffled and I take a second to stop. Look in the mirror.

Me. Monster-me. Me but not me.

And then I hear it.

'There's a tranny in there.'

I can almost feel the finger pointing.

I can see dark shapes moving through the gap under the door.

Whispers start.

All of a sudden I'm very very cold.

All of a sudden I'm very very aware of the tight binder elastic compressing my chest, my lungs, and when I hear it again –

'*Tranny.*'

All I can think is how easy it would be for them to pull me apart at the seams.

Whispers become words. The angry mob gathers.

I can't speak.

My mouth is stiff with rigor mortis.

Knocking.

I look in the mirror.

Banging. Battering ram.

Monsters are big. And scary.

'COME OUT! COME OUT!'

I'm small. And I'm scared.

Voices are louder now, louder banging louder, there's shouting, shouting and footstomps AND THEN THE GATE STARTS TO SPLINTER INWARDS –

Suddenly the door is open, the music of the party swells back and party lights burst in, spilling and flashing across the walls, filling the room.

Where are my friends?

'Monster.'

Can I just?

'MONSTER.'

I can see flickering red and – MONSTER – can someone –
BANG cracking breaking FIRE please – MONSTER – broken
bottles – louder harder MONSTER – CAN SOMEONE –
BANG SHOUTING LOUDER PITCHFORKS STAMPING
SCREAMING PLEADING FIRE FLICKER FIRE
PITCHFORK MONSTER FREAK SCREAMING MONSTER
FIRE MONSTER PITCHFORKS MONSTER MONSTER
MONSTER and I don't want to be a monster any more.

I don't want to be a monster any more.

He steps out of the scene.

I don't want to be a monster.

He begins yanking off his costume. He wipes off the paint.

I don't want to be a monster.

*He redresses in his clothes from before the party. They're softer,
baggier, safer.*

I don't want to be a monster.

*He goes to the costume he pulled off, selects a single piece of it,
maybe a jacket, and picks it up. He brushes it off, apologising to
it almost, and hangs it back up.*

*He takes a moment and then turns to face the audience. This
feels like something he's being very brave about doing.*

I don't want to be a monster.

Twelve

It's six a.m. It's the tenth of November, and I'm looking at
myself in the bathroom mirror.

The sun's not really up yet properly so everything is either a bit
grey or bleached yellow by my old side lamp.

It's a big day today. I've got my consultation. For chest surgery. Finally! Finally.

And Mia's going to come home for a few days tomorrow. We're going to hang out. She's promised.

It's still a bit weird.

We've talked on the phone a few times but when we do talk we don't talk about the party.

We don't talk about how Fizz found me outside crying, sat between two cars, how I tried to apologise through tears and hiccups and she quietly said 'It's fine, are you okay?' And I cried even harder until I was sick on the pavement.

We don't talk about how Mia came out to find us and when she saw my face, messy with tears, snot, a streak of blood, she exploded and Sophia had to drag her back out the house, spitting and swearing at the boys inside.

We don't talk about how she sat with me for hours in A and E, our hands clamped together in a white-knuckle grip between the plastic seats. And we don't talk about how we didn't talk the entire time we sat there waiting.

But I think tomorrow we will.

…

When I realised I was too excited to sleep last night I decided to watch *The Wolf Man*.

It felt a bit obvious. A man and a monster fighting for control over one body.

The werewolf gets shot in the end. He dies, and turns back into the man.

There's this thing that people say online, that people who hate trans people say online, about how once I die, and I rot away and all that's left of me is my bones, that 'they'll be able to tell'.

…

As if that means anything about what type of person I was.

If it walks like a man and talks like a man. If it laughs like a man, cries like a man and everyone who ever knew me and cared about me remembers me as a man then who the fuck cares if my bones have child bearing hips?

And I think the type of man I'd like to be remembered as is a good one. A man who has his shit together. Who was a good friend. The type of man who was proud to be himself.

I can't wait to see Mia tomorrow. I'm going to give her the biggest hug.

I look at myself in the mirror again.

I see me, but not me, but definitely definitely just me.

He says 'Hey, you're nearly a year on T.'

Later I tell Mum I'd like to go to my appointment by myself.

She asks me, like, nine times if I'm sure, if I'm going to be alright by myself, if I need her to – Mum. I think I just want to do this on my own.

'You're right, you're right. Just ring me. When you get there. And when you're out, let me know how it goes and make sure that you – ' *MUM!*

'No okay, you go. Be careful.'

I will. Can you pick me up after, from the station?

Love you.

'And I love you.'

The door clicks behind me, and I start to head off when I see someone, over the road and three doors down.

He takes out a flower.

She's there again.

Hi. Hello.

I wanted to talk to you. I know I look… a bit different recently, so I wanted to come and say hi, and that this is me now, and that I'm really happy. Or closer to it, or something, or it doesn't really matter because really I just wanted to say sorry. In case you didn't recognise me. In case I scared you.

But mostly I wanted to… introduce myself. Again.

'Is that flower for me?'

Yes.

'Are you a boy now?'

Uh, yeah.

'Well that's okay. Boys don't scare me.'

She smiles, then turns and runs inside, and the door swings shut behind her.

He is still for a moment, and then, a fond farewell:

Sensational.

Trans+ Support Networks

Below is a list of organisations who provide specialised support to trans, nonbinary, intersex, and any other gender diverse identity. These support services are UK wide.

TRUK Listens
Phone: 0800 009 0584
Open daily 8 a.m.–midnight

Mermaids
Phone: 0808 801 0400
Webchat: mermaidsuk.org.uk/support-line
Open Mon–Fri, 1–8.30 p.m.

Gendered Intelligence
Phone: 0800 640 8046
WhatsApp: 07592 650 496
Email: supportline@genderedintelligence.co.uk
Open weekdays at various times.

Mindline (Trans+ specific number)
Phone: 0300 330 5468
Open Fri evenings

TransUnite
Directory to find in-person Trans support groups across the UK
transunite.co.uk

Switchboard LGBT+ Helpline
Phone: 0800 0119 100
Email: hello@switchboard.lgbt
Webchat: switchboard.lgbt
Open daily 10 a.m.–10 p.m.

A Nick Hern Book

Dear Young Monster first published in Great Britain as a paperback original in 2025 by Nick Hern Books Limited, The Glasshouse, 49a Goldhawk Road, London W12 8QP

Dear Young Monster copyright © 2025 Pete MacHale

Pete MacHale has asserted his right to be identified as the author of this work

Cover photography by Finn Crawley, graphic design by Jackson Dean

Designed and typeset by Nick Hern Books, London
Printed in Great Britain by Mimeo Ltd, Huntingdon, Cambridgeshire PE29 6XX

A CIP catalogue record for this book is available from the British Library

ISBN 978 1 83904 499 1

www.nickhernbooks.co.uk/environmental-policy

Nick Hern Books' authorised representative in the EU is
Easy Access System Europe – Mustamäe tee 50, 10621 Tallinn, Estonia
email gpsr.requests@easproject.com